THE WAY IT IS

Tao Te Ching

Also by David Lindley

How to Write a Haiku
The Song of Myself: a new verse translation of The Bhagavad Gita
Something & Nothing: Selected Poems
The Freedom to Be Tragic
Ideas of Order
Book of Days

THE WAY IT IS

The Tao Te Ching

of

LAO TZU

A translation

by

David Lindley

I've been translating Lao Tzu. The result is not what I expected.
Leo Tolstoy, diary entry for 6th March 1884

Verborum Editions

© David Lindley

First published 2018 by Verborum Editions

www.verborumeditions.com

978-1-907100-06-2

INTRODUCTION

The Tao Te Ching and Lao Tzu
We do not know, and cannot know, the author of the Tao Te Ching, or indeed whether it is a work of a single author or a collection of sayings, teachings and, occasionally, interpolated commentary, compiled over an unknown length of time. Waley[1] dates it to late 3rd century BC on both philological grounds and on the internal evidence of references to contemporary philosophical writings and controversies which form the context of much of the argument of the Tao Te Ching. The traditional dating to the 6th century BC, contemporary with Confucius, is upheld by other scholars[2]. Ren Jiyu[3] also places the original teaching in the 6th century, suggesting it was then developed by disciples in following centuries. It does in any case belong to, or concerns itself with, a period of disorder, quite probably the so-called Warring States Period prior to the unification of the empire in 221 BC. The earliest 'inner' chapters of Chuang-tzu (4th century BC) are, in the view of A. C. Graham, uninfluenced by the Tao Te Ching which, he says, is 'not attested until late in the 3rd century BC.'[4] Wilhelm[5] bases his earlier dating on the evidence of the Chuang-tzu texts without making the distinctions in their evolution that Graham was subsequently able to do. On balance, mid to late 3rd century BC seems the most probable date for the work.

There are Chinese 'biographies' of Lao Tzu (whose name means 'old philosopher', a clue in itself to his merely representative character) but they are essentially legendary and lack historical evidence. (For a discussion of authorship in ancient China see Waley, Appendix 1 to his Introduction.) Yet any close reading of the original text does reveal a personality, a teacher personally and emotionally involved in a teaching that is also a way of life, continually at odds with a social and political order derived from a misunderstanding of the nature of power. For Lao Tzu, power is not 'exercised',

INTRODUCTION

as we observe it in the desire for material advantage, in conflicts of self-interest, in hierarchies of influence, in self-aggrandisement. This sort of power does not conquer the world, for the world cannot be conquered. All these illusory edifices, built on ignorance, ultimately fall back to earth. The only source of power is Tao, on which the world rests and therefore cannot fall, and the only way to live is in accord with Tao and its power (Te), which is not a power to be exercised but a virtue to be quietly conformed with. There is a sense, throughout the book, that though his philosophy is simple and though he feels quietly compelled to speak about what cannot be spoken of, he has little hope of changing men's natures beyond the possibility of changing one's own:

> *My words are very easy to understand*
> *and put into practice*
> *yet no one in the world understands them*
> *or puts them into practice.* [70]

Traditionally, the Tao Te Ching is divided into two parts: chapters 1-37 constitute the Tao Ching, the 'classic' or 'canon' (Ching) of the Tao; and the chapters that follow make up the Te Ching, the 'classic' of Te (power), though there is no strictly discernible divergence between the two parts. Together they are the Tao Te Ching: The Book of the Tao and the Te. Those two terms require some commentary.

Tao and Te

'Tao' means 'path' or 'way', and 'way' or 'The Way' is how it has generally come to be translated. But the way of what? In the context of the Tao Te Ching it sometimes seems to carry the meaning of the 'right' or 'true' way, in a moral sense, suggesting Dante's 'right way' that was lost to him in a dark wood of error and delusion; and sometimes it can suggest to our minds the words of Jesus (John 14:6): 'I am the way, the truth, and the life.' As a verb it carries the meaning of something spoken, so it is tempting to equate the Tao with *logos*, the 'Word', of St John ('In the beginning was the Word, and the Word was with God, and the Word was God') and to an extent it does bear the idea of the original commanding word, but one that is given of itself. Carus[6] defines it nicely as 'the excellent, the pure, and stirring word'. In a more general sense it is a way among other ways, a teaching among other teachings, the right way amidst a choice of wrong ways. But its essential meaning here is 'the way it is', 'the way things are', 'the way the world works' in and of itself, without words, without analysis, without commentary and, above all, without interference. If we think of it as the 'ultimate reality' we might do so in the words of Chuang Tzu as translated by Legge: 'If you could hide the world in the world, so that there was nowhere to which it could be removed, this would be the grand reality of the ever-enduring Thing.'[7] Apart from the unusual rendering of Tao as 'the way it is' in the opening verse, I have either left 'Tao' untranslated or chosen to use 'the way' when it seemed most natural to do so in the context, leaving further elucidation of its meaning to the notes and commentary.

'Te' as a concept is not particularly difficult to understand, but it presents difficulties for the translator because the two most appropriate word choices, 'virtue' and 'power', are both burdened with associations of meaning that detract from 'the excellent, the pure' word, 'Te'. I have generally settled for the word 'power', as Waley has done, though 'virtue' in its older meaning of an inherent energy or capacity would be better were it not for centuries of Christian idiomatic use to mean 'moral' virtue. 'Power', too, is unfortunate because we now associate power with the powerful: that is, with the exercise of power as a form of domination, control and coercion. Occasionally this is useful, for Lao Tzu contrasts the 'power' of the Tao with the power of men and the power of the state, both of which carry that meaning: the 'yielding' power of the Tao is very different from the 'wielding' of power by men. 'Te' has more the meaning of the generative and sustaining power we associate with nature, the 'acting without acting' of that something that is nothing, which Lao Tzu calls the Tao.

If we define the Tao, as we have done above, both as 'the way it is' and 'the way it works' the latter definition when coupled with the first captures the totality of the 'way'. The Tao is not one thing that 'is' and Te something it possesses. In this respect 'the way and *its* power' is misleading. The 'way' is something travelled, and you can't separate the way from the way it goes. It is the way it is by 'virtue' of the way it works. Tao and Te are really interchangeable rather than complementary terms, a convenience of language and syntax that allows us to speak on the one hand of the mysterious and unnameable nature of reality, the world hidden in the world, and on the other to illustrate how that same eternal, nebulous Tao magically and inexhaustibly produces the 'ten thousand things' of the phenomenal world, by speaking of the Tao as Te. A rough parallel might be to the idea of 'Nature' and the 'power' of Nature to put out leaves on the tree. We know these are merely concepts that help us express a meaning that transcends both. There is nothing in the world called 'Nature' that we can discover separate from 'its' natural power to bring things into being. When we say, 'Aren't the works of nature wonderful?' we are not really separating nature from *its* works other than as a figure of speech. Similarly, Te is the work, the action, the operation of Tao but not in the sense of one thing (Tao) exercising its power (Te), though in the text this is often the way the action of the Tao is expressed. The Tao 'acts without acting', and that action is Te. The Tao is both the way it is and the way it works.

The inherent power in all things
is derived solely from the Tao.
The Tao itself
is something elusive and indistinct,

> *so elusive and indistinct*
> *yet somehow latent in it*
> *are the forms of things...* [21]

The spirit of the valley

> *The valley spirit never dies.*
> *I call it the mysterious feminine...* [6]

Unlike the idea of God, who oversees the world, or Heaven, which is always above, the Tao is always 'below'. It is the source of all that is, the foundation upon which everything rests, the valley into which all waters flow, the beginning to which all living things return. It does not use its power to dominate or control the world. It uses its power to sustain the world. The desires of men and the ambitions of states are illusions destined to fail and fall, and when they fail they fall back to the source, for all forms of power that are not in accord with the Tao have no permanent foundation. Hence the Tao is described as weak, soft, yielding and, paradoxically, as empty but always full. These terms are the very opposite of the words we would normally associate with the idea of power. It is the feminine, the receptive, as opposed to the dominating male element, the low as opposed to the high. A recurring analogy is with water, both in the way it flows to the lowest point and as something soft and gentle but capable of wearing out stone and forming valleys:

> *In this world*
> *there is nothing softer or gentler*
> *than water*
> *yet no one*
> *pitting himself against the hard*
> *and the strong can do better.*
> *Nothing better exemplifies*
> *how weakness defeats strength*
> *and the gentle overcomes hardness...* [78]

INTRODUCTION

In what way can the low be more powerful than the high and mighty? How can weakness overcome strength? The Tao is the beginning of everything, the source, the eternal and unchanging nature of the world as it is, enfolded in itself. In the phenomenal world, everything changes, everything comes and goes. The Tao remains. Our striving in the world arises from self-interest, desire, ambition. We see this throughout the Tao Te Ching, when it speaks of people vying for position and advancement in the state bureaucracy, in their taste for fine food, in show-off dress, in the acquisition of wealth, in the state's pursuit of power both through diplomatic deception and through war. It asks why we should seek status when the desire for it makes us anxious and when we have it we become anxious about losing it. Why are we not content with plain food and simple clothing? If we accumulate jewels and jade we only create the opportunity for theft, and in ourselves the fear of losing what we have. War kills people, devastates the land that we should otherwise be cultivating. And time and death ensure that whatever we store up for ourselves will prove impermanent. If we understood this at the beginning, we would not venture far from the beginning. Strength is expended, that is all you can do with it:

> ...*the strongest tree*
> *is marked for felling...* [76]

Weakness rests in itself, the low receives everything. All the works of man take us off the path, the Way, the source to which they must all return. It waits for us. To harness the power of the Tao, we wait with it.

> *If you follow the Way*
> *you will be like the Way.*
> *If you harness its power*
> *you will act in accord with its power.* [23]

Tao, heaven, earth and man

To act in accordance with Tao and Te is described as 'acting without acting' or 'non-action' (*wu-wei*). The Tao is the source of heaven and earth and man but is not a power that rules over them, is not what we might call 'agency'. In the Tao Te Ching the ruling or determining agent, the natural cause of events in the world, is referred to as 'Heaven' (*t'ien*), which can broadly be interpreted as 'providence' – and when occurring in conjunction with 'Earth' as 'Heaven and Earth' it carries the meaning of 'Nature', the natural order of events in the world. While of course rooted in the mythology of the dwelling place of the gods and the abode of the dead, Heaven in this context is a more generalised concept: our fate and fortune and the reason why things turn out the way they do are not in our hands, but, as we might say (remembering our sacred relationship to the world that we think we have forgotten) 'in the lap of the gods'.

> *Who knows what the will of Heaven is*
> *in what it chooses?*
> *Even the wise man*
> *finds it hard*
> *to fathom a reason.* [73]

The 'Way of Heaven' evens things out. It raises the low and brings down the high (see Chapter 77). 'Heaven' appears several times in the Tao Te Ching, and often seems to be equated with the Tao itself. But we learn quite clearly in Chapter 25 how the Tao, Heaven, earth and man are connected:

> *Man follows the way of the earth.*
> *Earth follows the way of Heaven.*
> *Heaven follows the Tao.*
> *The Tao is what it is of itself*
> *and follows its own way.*

The Tao, the mysterious and unnameable Tao, is 'the mother of all things in heaven and earth'[25]. Heaven is not the Tao but it is the operant nature of the world that owes its existence to the 'formlessness' of the Tao. Heaven exists as the earth exists, formally, but their existence depends on something else, which is essentially formless. Heaven, of its nature, *must* follow the Tao, which is why the Tao Te Ching can speak of the Tao of Heaven and the Tao in the same breath. Just as Heaven is dependent on the Tao, the earth is dependent on Heaven (the underlying creation myth), and man is the creature of earth. These are the given fateful inter-relationships of man and the world, the way it is. But the way it is, the phenomenal and contingent nature of being, rests firmly on the way it *really* is, on the ever-enduring, ever productive and engendering but unknowable Tao.

Knowledge
The Tao is unknowable and unnameable. The knowable and the nameable are the 'ten thousand things' we ourselves have differentiated and detached from their essential oneness and original emptiness. How has that come about? Once we name the one as 'one', we have 'two', the one and the not-one, from which we derive the multiplicity of things we give our minds to. Why do we do this? Because we are led by our desires to possess things, utilise things, set one thing above another, beauty above ugliness, good above bad. It is only because we have separated one thing out from its unity that we have two, and it is only because we desire one thing above another that we are led astray from the true way into the ways of men.

The opening chapter nails this down:

> *It was from the nameless*
> *that heaven and earth*
> *came into being.*

INTRODUCTION

> *It was by the naming of names*
> *that the multiplicity of things*
> *came to be.*
>
> *Truly is it said that*
> *only he who frees himself*
> *from all desires*
> *sees the secret heart of things.*
> *He who never frees himself*
> *from his desires*
> *sees only their appearances.*

The point is pursued in the opening of the second chapter:

> *Only because everyone knows*
> *beauty as beauty*
> *is there ugliness.*
>
> *Only because everyone knows*
> *goodness as goodness*
> *is there evil.*

If we free ourselves from our desires we can rediscover the secret heart of things, the undifferentiated Tao. We do this by not interfering with the natural order of the world, as though we had some special knowledge or privileged right to change that order, or add to it, or correct it, or dominate it, to impose our will on it. The human order, the social order, the political order, are artificial constructs built on top of it. All our ideas, knowledge, innovations are simply an intellectual ordering of concepts that merely illustrates our own cleverness. They are words. And words, as we have learned, name things, differentiate things that are actually one, wordless and empty. What the world is and what we say about it are separate constellations. The right way to act is not to act, to leave things alone. By leaving things alone we align ourselves with the Tao, which acts without acting yet accomplishes everything.

> *This world is a sacred*
> *not a material thing.*
> *All action is harmful.*
> *If you try to seize hold of it*
> *you will lose it.* [29]

and

> *The Tao does not act*
> *yet everything is accomplished through it.* [37]

It is this fundamental idea that underlies the Tao Te Ching's attitude towards knowledge, knowledge as something added on, knowledge as cleverness, knowledge as an unnecessary complication of the world and life's essential simplicity, as just, in a phrase, more stuff.

We should see the Tao Te Ching's frequent attacks on knowledge and learning, invention, innovation and sophistication, in this light. The notion, in our modern age, that we might give up our computers and return to a simpler binary form of recording information by tying knots in string (see Chapter 80) will not strike us as realistic, but nonetheless it does allow us to rethink how much knowledge, how much information we really need to live a good life. The more things we have, the more we want; the greater our need for acquisition, the more we have to fear losing; the more we complicate our lives, the more stressed and unhappy we become. What is the point of 'progress', which is what Lao Tzu implies, if it takes us farther and farther away from peace and tranquillity? What is the point of distinguishing ourselves in the world when all that is worth having is to be at ease in it? Lao Tzu urges on us a return to an idealised simpler state of affairs without, I think, quite believing it could be accomplished. But that is not a reason for not recognising our over-complicated way of life for what it is: a complex of desires, wishes, dissatisfactions, hopes and illusions, burdening the 'secret heart of things' to which, when we have understood it, we are always able to return.

> *All is peace and contentment there,*
> *all is at rest.* [35]

Man and the state

The notion of that return to an ideal state of being is embodied in the ideal of the 'sage' (*sheng*), one who has harnessed the Te, a term which I have generally translated as the 'wise man'. Wilhelm defines him as 'the individual who, by putting away his individual inclinations and wishes, completely corresponds to the principle of Life [Tao].' He is, says Wilhelm, 'in a sense, a cosmic power.' The sage, however, is not simply a philosopher. He is at once an idealisation of a past 'golden age' when the world was ruled by wise men uncorrupted by desires and self-interest, and the ideal of the wise ruler whose rule is in accord with the Tao. 'Let us go back,' says Lao Tzu in the opening words of Chapter 80, having previously spoken of the 'ancients' and the 'old days'. A great ruler should be self-effacing, seeming to allow things to happen of their own accord – that is, to rule in accord with the Tao in the idealised ancient way.

> *Under a great ruler*
> *the people are scarcely aware of his rule....*
> *The wise ruler says little*
> *but accomplishes everything*
> *and lets everyone believe*
> *things just happen naturally.* [17]

He should not interfere:

INTRODUCTION

> *A ruler should always rule*
> *by not interfering.*
> *In fact, only by not interfering*
> *is he qualified to rule.* [48]

When the rule of the state accords with the Tao

> *The wise ruler will say:*
> *I practise the art of doing nothing*
> *and the people of their own accord conform.* [57]

The Tao Te Ching extols the way and its power using a variety of analogies to show how the weak overcomes the strong, the gentle and yielding brings about harmony; how desire and the pursuit of power are doomed to fail; how cleverness interferes with the natural scheme of things and the natural order of society. Its intention in doing so is less to provide a spiritual guide for everyman than advice to the ruler and a refutation of the traditional command structure of empire, its rules and laws and definitions and restrictions.

Given the main thesis that the harmony of society comes about by letting the people alone and not interfering by creating more and more rules for them to follow, not ruling top down through 'rewards and punishments', we might expect some argument in favour of letting the people rule themselves. That idea has never taken hold in China, from ancient times to today. There is always a state, or empire, and there must always be order in the state for disorder and discord are anathema both to the state and to its ordinary citizens. Not for a moment in the philosophy of the Tao Te Ching is there a suggestion that a state could order itself without the actions of a ruler and without the people's respect for the ruler. But the wise ruler should act without acting, rule without ruling (see Chapter 57) through an understanding of the Tao and the adoption of its power.

The ruler should not put himself above the people

but, in keeping with the lowly valley spirit of the Tao, desire nothing for himself and seek only the welfare of his people. Why would the most powerful person in the world create wealth for himself and not for the benefit of everyone else, and why would he want to be admired when his merit lies in what he quietly achieves and not in how ostentatiously he presents his public image?

> *The wise ruler creates wealth*
> *but desires nothing for himself.*
> *He deserves merit but asks for none.*
> *What need has he*
> *to draw attention to himself?* [77]

Life, for the ordinary person, the peasant, the farmer, the trader, is a burden. The wise ruler should not add to that burden by stirring up ambitions, by favouring some over others, by imposing rules and restrictions, by executing law breakers, by over-taxing and oppressing the people.

> *Don't fence them in.*
> *Don't make their lives a burden.*
>
> *They will not weary of life*
> *if you do not burden them.* [72]

Rather, his role is to make sure they are well-fed, he should 'strengthen their bones and fill their bellies' and not fill their heads with superfluous knowledge that leads only to restlessness, envy, dissatisfaction and, ultimately, to rebellion and disorder (see Chapter 3). The government should not try to regulate every aspect of their lives. Ideally, the ruler should not interfere and should let the lives of the people follow their natural, if harsh, course in accordance with the eternal law of the Tao.

Realism and idealism

There is an undercurrent of pessimism in Lao Tzu's philosophy of the Tao and the Te. The Tao is easy to understand, he says, but no one in the world understands it or acts upon it (see Chapter 70).

> *Few there are who understand*
> *the value of a teaching without words,*
> *of acting without acting.* [43]

He is, he says at one point in the text where he seems to reveal his own personality, a perpetual outsider, at odds with the world because he is at one with the Tao from which the rest of humanity has become estranged:

> *I am adrift*
> *as though I don't belong anywhere.*
> *… I'm like the sea*
> *endlessly drifting.*
> *Everyone else has something to do.*
> *I saunter along aimlessly*
> *like a vagabond.* [20]

His idealistic philosophy is always a counter to the reality of life: the self-interests and egoism of men, the arrogance and selfishness of the ruling class, the limited horizons of the ruled, the hardships of everyday life, the instability of the social order, the rise and fall of the powerful, the violence and destruction of countries at war, the delusion of immortality. Real power, real 'immortality', lies with Te. And this real power should be applied to all aspects of governance, statecraft and warfare. The Tao Te Ching decries violence and war and the misuse of power, but does not seem to hold out a realistic expectation that any of it will end. We are no longer living in that former age, at the beginning of time, when men lived in harmony with the Tao. No one now understands, and no one practises this teaching. Yet it must be taught, for while this teaching may be idealistic in terms of the likelihood that the characters of men can be changed, the true way is all that is worth speaking about. So we see that the advice given to the ruler acknowledges the realities and circumstances that confront the state and its enemies, and applies the principles of Tao and Te to actions that will return the world to harmony.

Ideally, the ruler should not hold the empire by force of arms, for violence is returned with violence and the land laid desolate. If war is necessary, then only necessary actions should be pursued (see Chapter 30).

> *To a man who is master of himself*
> *weapons are evil things*
> *and not instruments of his own will.*
> *He uses them only because it is unavoidable.* [31]

He should not celebrate his victories but formally mourn those whose lives he has taken, for

> *... one who delights in slaughter*
> *will never achieve anything worthwhile*
> *in this world.* [31]

Conflict has to be conducted with detachment, without passion. War is a necessary evil to be undertaken with compassion, with the least harm, the least violence. Although such violence is contrary to the Tao, the principles and arts of war are derived from the same philosophy that teaches strength through weakness, leadership through submission, success by giving way.

> *One who understands the art of war says:*
> *I did not invite it,*
> *I am simply a guest.*

> *I would not advance an inch,*
> *but rather retreat a foot.*
>
> *This is called:*
> *going off to war without marching,*
> *threatening without raising a hand,*
> *opposing without enmity,*
> *arming without arms.* [69]

The simple but enigmatic Tao is eternal, everything else is impermanent. Tao is the persistent reality that underlies all realities built upon it: the multiplicity of things we have separated out from the eternal, nameless, unknowable principle and given names to and which have become the source of all our contradictions and contentions – what we love and what we hate, our self-regard and our despite of others, our desires and dissatisfactions, our will to power and advantage, our greed and our possessiveness, our lust for life that takes no regard of the reality of our mortality and the temporality of all that we have and all that we think we are. The Tao cannot be spoken of, but of course Lao Tzu *does* speak of it, knowing full well that all our troubles stem from words, from what we have constructed for ourselves on the foundation of the wordless, to which everything ultimately returns.

A note on the translation
The text of the Tao Te Ching is essentially a sequence of simple statements, for the most part unelaborated and unexplained. Their simplicity can't always be equated with clarity. Much is compacted into a few Chinese characters: variants on statements from other scholarly or historical texts; oblique references to contemporary philosophical and moral perspectives; figurative associations with traditional folk beliefs, rites and ceremonies; all within a context of a social, political, military and administrative structure in

INTRODUCTION

a distant and unfamiliar past. Add to these factors further uncertainties of the meaning of individual characters, plays on words, syntactical ambiguity and possible errors and distortions in the received text, any attempt to transfer (somewhat different from translating) the Chinese text to an equivalent English notation is bound to fail.

Some parts of the text are written in verse – that is, when allowance is made for changes in tonality over the centuries, some of the words rhyme. Some attempts have been made to translate these passages into rhymed couplets, without success. Legge's otherwise valuable translation and commentary is a particularly dismal effort. The condensed meaning of each statement is obscure enough without the added strain of trying to fit those statements into English jingles.

Many of the chapters contain repeated, balanced statements conjoined by a word or phrase that is usually translated as 'therefore'. A literal translation of such a passage from Chapter 71 would be, 'Only when we are sick of sickness are we therefore not sick. The sage is not sick because he is sick of sickness, therefore he is not sick.' The expression for 'therefore' occurs more than 90 times, by my count, throughout a text of only 81 short chapters. In translation, it is often redundant; and where translated it can be misleading, since we expect what follows it to be a logical consequence of the previous statement. But it is rarely so: 'Only when people are not burdened are they not burdened, *therefore* the sage knows himself but does not think highly of himself.' [72]

All this sets the challenge of being concise in finding an English medium while making oneself clear. In the last quoted passage, to translate it as it literally appears in the text as, 'Only when not burdened are they not burdened' would answer for concision but would leave the meaning still to be extracted – in other words, the task of translation would be left to the reader (as may well have been intended

INTRODUCTION

in the Tao Te Ching's contemporary scholarly context and the audience to whom it may have been addressed). So the wording becomes:

> *Don't make their lives a burden.*
> *They will not weary of life*
> *if you do not burden them.*

My priority has been to make the text and its meaning clear, without saying more than is needed and without imposing what Wilhelm, even as far back as 1910, criticised as the translator's 'intuitive interpretation' of it. This translation is neither verse nor prose. It is rather a series of linked statements, with line arrangements that help both separate and link ideas. Some of those statements are more formal than others, and where I have detected a personal and conversational tone for some of those ideas, I have adopted a more relaxed style.

The division of the text into two parts, and into 81 sections with chapter titles, is how the Tao Te Ching has come down to us (there are other variants of the text and its divisions). The titles traditionally ascribed to each chapter are not always helpful and have usually been ignored in later translations. I have created chapter titles of my own for this translation that seem to me to best reflect the essence of each chapter.

Finally, I have chosen not to adopt the pinyin standard for the romanisation of Chinese characters, which has been internationally adopted since the 1980's. All the texts I have used or referred to, and all the current translations in English of any value, with one exception, predate the new standard. I see no purpose to be served in recasting the ubiquitous 'Tao' as 'Dao' and the Tao Te Ching as the Dao De Jing, and ignoring the long, unstandardised history of our love affair with this much read and much translated classic.

INTRODUCTION

[1] Waley, Arthur. *The Way and Its Power*. London, 1934
[2] Chan, Wing-tsit. *The Natural Way of Lao Tzu* in *A Source Book in Chinese Philosophy*. Princeton, 1963
[3] Ren, Jiyu. *The Book of Lao Zi*. Beijing, 1993
[4] Graham, A. C. *Chuang-tzu, The Seven Inner Chapters and other writings from the book Chuang-tzu*. London, 1981
[5] Wilhelm, Richard. *Lao-tzu, Tao the king: das Buch des Alten vom Sinn und Leben*. Jena, 1910
[6] Carus, Paul. *Lao-tze's Tao-Teh-King*. London & Chicago, 1898
[7] Legge, James. *The Texts of Taoism (Part 1)*. Oxford, 1891

THE WAY IT IS

Tao Te Ching

1

The Eternal and Unnameable Tao

The way it is
that can be spoken of
is not the way
it really is.
The name that can be named
is not the name of it.

It was from the nameless
that heaven and earth
came into being.
It was by the naming of names
that the multiplicity of things
came to be.

Truly is it said that
only he who frees himself
from all desires
sees the secret heart of things.
He who never frees himself
from his desires
sees only their appearances.

These are two different things,
originating from one sameness,
one with a name
and one without a name.

I call this sameness a mystery,
the mystery of mysteries,
the door to the secret heart of things.

Notes and commentary
The Tao Te Ching opens by immediately making the distinction between the unnameable Tao, the essence of the working of the universe, and every attempt at defining or finding a name for it. As soon as we name it, define it, describe it, attribute it to some power or reason, we are not in fact speaking of the Tao but simply using words. The world came into being out of that namelessness, and in essence remains nameless – *noumenal*, to use the Kantian term, a thing in itself. The *phenomenal* world is a mental construct. We name things, therefore they are what we name them. Why do we name them? Because we have an interest in them, because they are useful to us, because we are attached to them, because they are the objects of our material desires as material beings. Our desires and the phenomenal world, the world of appearances, are intertwined. The Tao is indefinable and nameless, and also desireless. Therefore we can only get an understanding of the real nature of the world and our actions in the world by freeing ourselves from our desires and attachments. If we can do that, then the door to the secret heart of things, the Tao, is open. The named and the nameless are really one and the same, originating from one source. It is just that we have mistaken our own definition of the world, our names for things, for the world itself.

2

The Order of Things

Only because everyone knows
beauty as beauty
is there ugliness.

Only because everyone knows
goodness as goodness
is there evil.

Likewise,
being and nothingness
give rise to each other,
difficult and easy,
long and short,
high and low,
are mutually dependent,
the voice and its tones harmonise,
and front and back
naturally go everywhere together.

Since this is so
the wise man acts by letting things alone
and teaches by saying nothing.

Whatever comes along
he accepts.

He does not own
what he creates.
He acts without self-interest.
He expects no thanks
for doing good.

He expects no reward.
How rewarding!

Notes and commentary
The theme of 'sameness' continues in Chapter 2. Nothing in reality is beautiful or good. They are names for our own preferences, and as soon as we distinguish one as more desirable, the other, less desirable, comes into being literally 'by definition'. Similarly, if something is long or high, then there must be something short or low. The named and the nameless are really one and the same, but we act in relation to the surface appearance of things, out of self-interest. The wise man, the sage, the man who acts in accord with the Tao, is without desire and lets things alone. He 'acts without acting' (*wu-wei*) in the conduct of his affairs, just as the Tao does. What he teaches is not defined by words, for words belong to appearances and the fragmentation of the nameless reality that gave rise to them. The Tao has no partisan interests, and nor does the man who acts in accord with it.

the voice and its tones harmonise. These harmonising dependencies refer to the tonal characteristics of the Chinese spoken language. 'Sound' is not separable from 'voice', any more than 'front' is separable from 'back'.

3

Ruling the Restless Heart

By not making one superior to another
we put an end to rivalry.

By putting no value on valuable things
we put an end to theft.

By not displaying things
when seen the heart at once desires
then hearts are undisturbed.

So the wise man rules the people
as the saying is
by emptying their heads
and filling their bellies,
weakening their wants
and strengthening their spines.

He gives no cause for scheming and ambition
and without a cause
would-be schemers have no cause to act.

By following the rule
of ruling without ruling
nothing is not ruled.

Notes and commentary
ruling without ruling. Wu-wei, non-action. By leaving things undisturbed, removing the sources of desire and individual ambition but providing for the welfare of the people, order is preserved.

4

The Unfathomable Source

The Tao is empty
but never exhausted,
the unfathomable source
of everything.

It is there
that all sharpness is blunted,
all tangles untangled,
harsh light softened,
and the dust of the world
settled.

Hidden in its own depths
it can only seem to be.
I do not know its origin.
It is the image of the world
before God.

Notes and commentary
The second verse of this chapter recurs in Chapter 56.

the image of the world before God. This is the only place in the Tao Te Ching where we might be justified in using the word 'God' for the sake of understanding. Literally, the reference is to the 'first ancestor', the creator and separator of heaven and earth, therefore the creator or first interferer in the original but unoriginated formless form of the world. Interestingly, Isaac Bashevis Singer, in his story *The Death of Methuselah*, called God an intruder who 'defiled the world with light and life'. There was a world before creation. That world, yet undivided, 'hidden in its own depths', is described in these words in the *Hymn to Creation* in the *Rig Veda* (10:129):

*There was nothing to divide
the day from night.
Then there was only
THAT
without breath,
breathed of itself,
the one,
and nothing beyond.
Then there was darkness
hidden in darkness…*

5

Emptiness

Nature is indifferent to man.
It treats everything under heaven
as straw dogs for the fire.
Why, then, should the wise ruler
show partiality to straw men?

Isn't the space
between heaven and earth
like a bellows, always empty
but at the same time inexhaustible,
always at work
producing more and more?

But empty words
are soon exhausted.
Best to keep your heart
within your heart.

Notes and commentary
straw dogs. Ritual sacrificial objects.

Nature is not benevolent and has no plan for us, yet everything is perfectly, if ruthlessly, well-ordered. The ruler/sage emulates the order of nature which, empty of all intention, continues inexhaustibly to create and sustain all things in heaven and earth. Words and controversies, in contrast, exhaust themselves.

6

The Mysterious Feminine

The valley spirit never dies.
I call it the mysterious feminine.
The opening of the mysterious feminine
I call the root of heaven and earth.

It exists and exists without form
yet we draw everything from it
ceaselessly and without effort.

Notes and commentary
The Tao that is inexhaustible is like a valley, an analogy that recurs throughout the Tao Te Ching. It is the eternal feminine from which everything is born. It is the receptive and submissive, the source, in contrast to the assertive, intrusive male element, and the high and mighty hills. It is hidden beneath and between and below, the formless obverse of the forms of things.

7

Life Without Ends

Heaven and earth endure for ever.
Is this because they don't exist for their own ends
and therefore have no end?

The wise man considers himself last
and so is considered first among men.
He has no particular concern for himself
yet manages to go on living.

Isn't it just because he's not self-interested
that all his interests are taken care of?

8

Natural Foundations

The highest good is like water.
It benefits all living things
yet is content to inhabit lowly places
men avoid.
In this way it resembles the Tao.

A house sits on level ground,
the heart has its profundities,
generosity requires deep humanity,
words must spring from the truth,
good government is founded on good order,
deeds on men's abilities,
and actions on the right time to act.

In every instance nothing gets above itself
and so nothing needs correcting.

Notes and commentary
In this chapter we encounter further analogies representing the nature of the Tao. Universal benevolence is like water, which benefits every living creature, and so resembles the Tao. Water always finds the lowest level yet man despises lowliness and seeks to rise above it. But everything has it foundations on something lower than itself. The key to understanding this chapter is in the words 'nothing gets above itself'.

9

Enough

Better to stop in time
than overfill the bucket!
If you're forever
sharpening a knife
it will soon wear out.

Once you've filled your house
with gold and jewels
who's going to protect it?

Wealth and status
lead to arrogance
and pride leads to a fall.

When your work is done
it's done. Leave it.
It's not about you
and your reputation.

This is the way of Heaven.

10

The Discipline of Unity

Can your wandering spirit
hold fast to the one?
Can you control your vital breath
and breathe as softly as a baby?

Can you purify your vision
of a profound mystery,
keep it clear and not falter?

In ruling the people
and governing the state
can you practise the art of non-action?
Just let the gates of Heaven open and close
like a bird feeding her young.

Can you penetrate to the heart of things
but seem as though you know nothing?

To help them live, to feed them,
but not to attribute that to yourself,
to act but not take credit for your actions,
to bring them up but not rule them with a rod of iron:
this is a deep and mysterious power.

Notes and commentary
The first part of this chapter refers to the techniques of Taoist *yoga*, controlling the mind to stop it wandering off into the realm of the senses and worldly desires, holding on instead to the 'one' which naturally comes in and out of vision and needs discipline to keep in focus. Breath control is an aid to quieting the mind, learning to breathe as softly and naturally as a baby. This leads on to the parallel that governing the

people should also be natural, like a bird simply feeding its young, letting things alone to open and close, ebb and flow. To be wise is to understand the mystery of the Tao, but that understanding does not lead to greatness or to the exercise of power, but to the ability to 'act without acting' – and to know without seeming to know.

11

Useful Emptiness

Thirty spokes around a hub
make a wheel,
but it's the empty axle hole
that lets it work.
We make a pot from clay,
but it's the empty space in it
that makes it useful.
We make doors
and windows in a house,
but it's the space that's useful.

Thus, useful things exist
as things
but their usefulness depends
upon the non-existent.

12

This and That

Colour blinds the eye,
music deafens the ear,
flavour deadens the palate,
hunting and chasing madden the mind,
and possessions tie you down.

And so the wise man
turns to that which is within
and turns away from outer things,
preferring this to that.

Notes and commentary
We are distracted by the external, and lose sight of the 'one' (see Chapter 10). 'This' is used here, as in later chapters, to stand for an inner understanding of the Tao, and 'that' for worldly attachments we should reject.

13

The Trouble with Self-esteem

Favour is as much a source of trouble as disgrace.
Self-esteem is painful to the self.

What is meant by the saying:
'Favour is as much a source of trouble as disgrace?'

We are as anxious about winning it
as we are fearful of losing it.
That's what it means.

What is meant by the saying:
'Self-esteem is painful to the self?'

The only reason why we suffer is
we have a self.
If we had no self
what could we fear
from either winning or losing?
That's what it means.

And so this saying, in a way, is also true:
One who esteems the people as himself,
one who loves the people as he loves himself,
can be entrusted with the state.

Notes and commentary
This chapter is a commentary on the source of pain and anxiety. We suffer only because we are unable to detach ourselves from our desires, hopes and ambitions. If we had no regard for our self – for status or reputation – but simply selflessly performed our duties, then the source of our troubles would disappear. The saying quoted here in

the last three lines is a fairly conventional statement of a moral philosophy that seems close to 'love thy neighbour as thyself', but actually means it is self-evident that the ruler will cultivate his own interests and should cultivate the interests of the people likewise. In the context, the saying is used to support the entirely opposite philosophy: one who has no regard for himself and therefore similarly does not promote the interests of individuals or factions is the one best fitted to rule the state.

14

The Tao

Look for it
and it can't be seen.
Its name is
the invisible one.

Listen for it
and it can't be heard.
Its name is
the silent one.

Reach for it
and it can't be grasped.
Its name is
the formless one.

Of these three
there is nothing to be said.
They merge into the single one.

It neither rises
into the light
nor sinks
into darkness.

Ceaseless and unnameable
it continuously arises,
always on its way back
to nothingness.

Its shape is shapeless,
its form formless,
its semblance merely seeming.

Meeting it
we can't see its face,
following it
we can't see its back.

To hold fast to the way of old
is to master the present,
to know its beginning
is to unravel the Tao's invisible thread.

Notes and commentary
The Tao is invisible, soundless, formless. Since there is nothing more to be said about any of these aspects, they should not be considered 'aspects' but 'one' (see Chapter 2). The Tao is ceaseless and inexhaustible. It is the original source, not merely historically as the beginning of the universe, but here and now. It is the everlasting beginning. It is ancient, and the ancients understood it. An invisible thread connects the present to the past, phenomena to their underlying non-existence, the 'ten thousand things' to the nameless.

15

The Old Masters

In the old days
those who had mastered the Tao
had a subtle and insightful
understanding of its mystery.
Since that understanding
is profound and hard to fathom
all I can do is speak of their outward behaviour.

They acted cautiously,
as one crossing a stream in winter,
prudently, as one considering
the dangers that lie all around,
reserved and respectful,
befitting a guest in this world.
They were willing to give way,
like ice beginning to melt,
plain and natural
like a block of uncarved wood,
receptive, like a valley among the hills,
absorbing all that came their way
like a muddy river.

Who can assume the world's murkiness
and by stilling it make it clear?
Who can keep that stillness for long
before the stir of things begins again?

Those who follow the Tao
do not seek to fill themselves to the brim
only to overflow, exhausted.

Notes and commentary
The text pictures an ideal age in which the 'ancients' understood and were at one with the Tao. This, it says, is how they behaved. At the end of the chapter it advocates a stilling of the mind through meditation, and warns against filling oneself with everything one can grasp, only eventually to lose it – in contrast to the Tao, which supplies everything yet never exhausts itself (see Chapter 9).

16

The Eternal Return

Attain to complete emptiness,
hold on to complete stillness.

Because I know all things arise
I know that they return.

Everything that flourishes
returns to its root.

Returning to the root
means returning to stillness.

To return to stillness
is to accept our fatality.

To accept our fate
is to acknowledge an eternal law.

To know the eternal
is to be enlightened.

To act in ignorance of the eternal
is to act recklessly.

When we know the eternal
we can find the capacity to embrace all
and by embracing all
we become inclusive and impartial.

To be inclusive and impartial
is to be princely
and to be princely

is to be ruled by Heaven.

To be ruled by Heaven
is to be subject to the Tao

and the Tao lasts for ever.

Although we are mortal
we do not suffer our mortality.

Notes and commentary
we do not suffer our mortality. If we embrace the everlasting beginning, if we live perpetually in eternity, at the still centre of our being, at one with the Tao, then although we are mortal, as bodies that return to their beginning, our lives are never in danger, we do not suffer our mortality, because we have never let go of the beginning.

17

Ruling by Not Ruling

Under a great ruler
the people are scarcely aware of his rule.
A lesser ruler they love and praise,
the lesser still they fear
and the least of all they despise.

So it is said:
If you don't have faith in people
they will not have faith in you.

The wise ruler says little
but accomplishes everything
and lets everyone believe
things just happen naturally.

18

Natural Harmony

It was when the Great Way declined
that we first came to speak about
human rights and moral obligations.
When astuteness and cleverness appeared
the Great Lie followed.
When families no longer lived in harmony
it was then we began to talk of
love and the duties of children.
When the country starts to fall apart
only then do we hear about
the need for loyalty and unity in government.

Notes and commentary
In ancient times, the idealised golden age, men lived in harmony with the Tao, the Great Way, without the need for laws, rules of conduct, moral codes. Once the Great Way declined, then society invented rights and obligations to be adhered to. When people abandoned simple living and became clever, devious, cunning, then hypocrisy, or the Great Lie, followed. Families in those days naturally lived in harmony. Only when that natural harmony was lost did the need arise for (Confucian) family values and duties to be spelled out. When the country starts to fall apart through mismanagement, suddenly we are asked for our loyalty, for national unity etc.

19

The Virtue of Simple Affections

If we got rid of wisdom and learning
people would be a hundred times better off.
If we stopped this business of
human rights and moral obligations
people would return
to their natural affections and duties.
If we gave up accumulating new things
there would be no more robbers and thieves.

But this is plain living,
and plainly not enough,
and since people must have
something to cling to,
let that be:

plainness itself,
simplicity,
selflessness and few desires.

20

A Fool at Heart

If you give up the social niceties
you've learned
you won't worry about saying OK instead of yes
in polite company.
It's not as though the difference
is a choice between good and evil.

Must I always worry
about what everyone else
worries about?

There's no end to this nonsense.

'Always merry and bright'
is how I would describe other people,
always off to one festival or another.

I alone seem indifferent to it all
like a newborn baby
who hasn't yet taken an interest in anything,
who hasn't yet learned to smile.

I am adrift
as though I don't belong anywhere.
Others have more than enough
but I seem to have nothing.

I'm a fool at heart
with an empty head!

They all seem so bright and lively
and so sure of themselves

while I'm so dull and uncertain.

I'm like the sea
endlessly drifting.
Everyone else has something to do.
I saunter along aimlessly
like a vagabond.

I can't live like they do.
I have never left
my mother's breast.

Notes and commentary
This is the most 'personal' of the chapters in the Tao Te Ching. The opening lines continue the theme of the preceding two chapters which urge abandoning rules of behaviour imposed on people's essential simplicity. Many of the codes of behaviour are social and ceremonial. In China there were different words for 'yes' and 'no' depending on the occasion and relative status. We might think of the 'shock' to middle class sensibilities of a guest using the wrong fork at dinner. Lao Tzu says, it's not as though we are choosing between good and evil.

I have never left my mother's breast. This echoes the earlier statement that he is like a newborn baby. He means that he takes his nourishment from the Tao, the mother of all things, and has never lost that attachment. Others are more concerned with social opinion, being busy and having a good time.

21

The Way and Its Power

The inherent power in all things
is derived solely from the Tao.
The Tao itself
is something elusive and indistinct,
so elusive and indistinct
yet somehow latent in it
are the forms of things,
still elusive and indistinct,
and the substance of things,
still shadowy and imperceptible,
and the spirit of things,
which is nonetheless very real and evident.

For never, from ancient times until now,
did anything forget its instructions,
and from that evidence
I can trace everything back to its source.
How do I know
that these are the ways of creation?

By this!

Notes and commentary

There is a mysterious power (Te) inherent in everything, a power that in the abstract we might call 'nature'. But nature is not identifiable as anything in particular. It is the spirit of things, and although we can't separate it from things themselves, it is clearly evident in those things. Everything is dependent on something that preceded it, without needing any instructions. That is what we mean by nature. If we trace things back to the source, we arrive at the original emptiness of the Tao. How can we know this is so? By this! By the evidence itself and the fact of Tao (see Chapter 12).

And so it's Spring again   so what
The leaves are leaves again   no tree forgot
Gregory Corso, *Reflections in a Green Arena*

22

Wholeness

To remain whole, give way.
To remain unbroken, bend.

To be empty is to be filled,
to be worn out is to be renewed.

To know little is to learn much,
to know too much is to become confused.
Therefore the wise man sticks to the one
and uses it to determine everything under heaven.

He does not show himself
therefore he is seen everywhere.
He does not distinguish himself
therefore he is distinguished.
He does not boast of himself
therefore he is admired.
Nor does he boast of his works
and so they endure.
He contends with no one
so no one in the world opposes him.

The old saying:
To remain whole, give way
remains true
for true wholeness
is a returning.

23

Losing the Way

To say little is to be like nature itself
for a storm does not last all morning
nor a downpour last all day.
What causes this? Heaven and earth.
If even nature can't sustain
its outpourings for long
how much less can man?

If you follow the Way
you will be like the Way.
If you harness its power
you will act in accord with its power.

If you act without it
then you've lost it.
When you conform to the Way
it will lend you its power,
when you go along with its power
it will lend you more power.
If you don't, it won't!

As I said before:
If you don't have faith in it
it won't have faith in you.

Notes and commentary
As I said before. I have added this phrase to maintain the colloquial style. The words that follow are identical to those in Chapter 17.

24

More Than Enough Is Too Much

He who stretches out on tiptoe
becomes unsteady.
He who takes the longest strides
does not walk any faster.

One who regards only himself
is not worthy of regard.
One who sets himself apart
is not thereby distinguished.
One who is already full of himself
has no more room to grow.

All this from the point of view of the Tao
is like leftover food that nobody wants
or a fester on the body
no one can stomach.
The Taoist turns away from it all.

25

The Great Tao

There was something formless
but sufficient in itself
that existed before heaven and earth,
silent, still, and without substance,
dependent on nothing else,
ceaseless and unchanging,
eternal and unfailing.

We might call it the mother
of all things in heaven and earth.
I do not know its name
but I call it the Tao.

If I had to find another name for it
I would call it 'The Great'.

To be great
means to be extensive,
to be extensive
means to extend to the farthest limits,
extending to the farthest limits
means returning to the beginning.

In this meaning the Tao is 'Great'.
Heaven has this greatness.
Earth has this greatness.
Man's world too has this greatness.

There are four great realms
and one is the realm of man:
Man follows the way of the earth.
Earth follows the way of Heaven.

Heaven follows the Tao.
The Tao is what it is of itself
and follows its own way.

Notes and commentary
The Tao is not something phenomenal that we can identify. Its greatness is described as extensive, and its extensiveness as limitless. Because it is everywhere, and always, to describe it as extending to its limits is to describe it as returning to its beginning. The great realms of man, earth, Heaven are aligned with or dependent on the Tao, which is not dependent on anything else but is what it is in itself.

26

The Dignity of Authority

Weightiness
is the foundation of lightness,
stillness
is the master of action.

Hence the truth of the saying:
A man of substance travelling
throughout the whole day
will never lose sight
of his weighty baggage cart
and despite magnificent distractions
along the way he sits still
and quiet and unconcerned.

How unfitting is it then
for a ruler in command
of ten thousand chariots
to take himself lightly
in full view of his empire?

To act lightly
is to forget the weightiness
that is the foundation of his office.
To act rashly
is to lose his authority.

Notes and commentary
This is advice to the ruler based on the principles of the Tao whose centre is still and actionless. The office of the ruler, the emperor, the president is a weighty and dignified one. If he seems to act lightly, with a light hand, he can do this because he takes his office seriously. Similarly, stillness

is the foundation of action, of 'acting without acting'. He is like the 'man of substance' who never loses sight of his responsibilities and is never distracted from his main purpose. But to act lightly, frivolously, rashly, in full view of the world, is to betray his office, lose his authority, and look like a fool.

27

Teaching the Tao

Perfect actions, like skilful travellers,
leave no tracks.
A good speaker makes no slips.
Good mathematicians do not need
to show their workings out.
Good locksmiths use no bolts or keys
yet no one can open their locks.
Skilful fastening is done
without rope or knots
yet can't be undone.

And so the wise man
always supports everyone
with the same perfect skill,
for no one is useless.
In the same way
he conserves everything,
because nothing is useless.
This is known as
acting in the hidden light of understanding.

The perfect man is the teacher
of the imperfect
and the imperfect
is the material of perfection.
If the teacher is not respected
and the imperfect is not valued
even the most intelligent observer
will misunderstand
the essential secret of the Tao.

Notes and commentary
Waley suggests that this chapter is a rebuttal of the critics of Taoist preoccupation with self-development over the heads of those with little understanding. The Tao, after all, is said to be a teaching without words (see Chapter 43) too inwardly focused to be of use to anyone else. But this is not so, it is just that the skill of teaching is hidden from view, even from the intelligent observer or critic. It would be wrong to dismiss the value of the teacher because you can't understand his usefulness as much as it would be wrong to disparage the ignorant as useless.

28

Returning to Simplicity

The man who knows full well his maleness
but holds on to the feminine
is like a deep valley in this world,
a valley from which the eternal power
never flows away.
He returns to the simplicity of a child.

He who lives by his own light
but is content with obscurity
is a model of the world.
Being a model of the world
the eternal power never fails him.
He returns to the limitless.

He who is honourable
but keeps his humility
is a channel for the world's eternal power.
He returns to the simplicity of uncarved wood.

Just as we carve the simplicity of wood
into useful objects
a wise ruler divides his own simplicity
among useful subjects,
his chiefs and officers,
but he stops there
and does not keep on cutting.

Notes and commentary

the simplicity of uncarved wood. The 'uncarved block' is an analogy that recurs in a number of places to stand for the original 'material' of the Tao in its essential and unadulterated simplicity before we make 'useful' things out of it. People in charge under the ruler should be carved, as it were, out of that same simplicity, but not made too much of. That simplicity is also associated with the simplicity of a child (the same expression used in Chapter 20, translated there as 'a newborn baby').

29

In Praise of Letting Things Alone

I have seen those
who want to take over the world
and do as they will with it
fail.
This world is a sacred
not a material thing.
All action is harmful.
If you try to seize hold of it
you will lose it.

Among people,
some lead and others follow,
some blow hot and some blow cold,
some are strong and others weak,
some succeed and others are defeated.

The wise man gives up
all extremes, excesses, self-indulgence.

Notes and commentary
You can't get hold of anything in this world because you can't separate out one thing from another. People strive to hold on to a permanent advantage, but thoughtful observation of the realities of this world shows that you can't get away from polar opposites. An extreme position is not an absolute position. You can ally yourself with the whole of it or suffer defeat in attempting to possess one aspect of it.

30

The Harvest of War

He who advises a ruler
in the way of the Tao
should advise him
not to hold the empire
by force of arms.
For the violent will suffer violence
in return.

Wherever a great army has been
thorns and brambles grow up
and bad harvests follow.

A good general strikes a decisive blow
then stops without pursuing his victory.
Nor does he glory in his actions
or boast of them or take pride in them
but acts only out of necessity
without unnecessary violence.

For the height of power
is followed by decline.

This is not the way of the Tao
and what is contrary to the Tao
simply comes to an end.

Notes and commentary
For the height of power is followed by decline. The principle of the Tao is that it is always returning, returning to the eternal beginning. All opposites revert. As we have noted in the previous chapter, any attempt to establish oneself at one extreme, as though it were an absolute in itself, is bound to

fail. What rises must fall, must come to an end.

31

We Should Mourn Our Victories

Even the finest arms are evil things
and the man of culture avoids them.
In time of peace he's a man of the left,
in time of war a man of the right.

To a man who is master of himself
weapons are evil things
and not instruments of his own will.
He uses them only because it is unavoidable.

He values peace and quiet
and takes no pleasure in victories.
If he were to take pleasure in his victories
it would be the same as delighting
in the slaughter of men
and one who delights in slaughter
will never achieve anything worthwhile
in this world.

In good times we respect the left,
in bad times we turn to the right.
Then, the low ranking general will sit on the left,
the high ranking general will sit on the right.
This is the same protocol we see at a funeral.
And just as we mourn the dead
we should mourn the slaughtered
and the victor should be the chief mourner.

Notes and commentary
The general consensus is that a later commentary has been assimilated into the original text of this chapter. While stylistically different from other parts of the Tao Te Ching, it

is nonetheless in keeping with the argument in the preceding chapter. The references to 'left' and 'right' probably relate to (now obscure) court protocols and the formal ranking of advisers to the ruler in times of war and times of peace. They accidentally conform a little to our own concepts of right wing and left wing positions. The ancient protocols are said to be the same as they are for funerals, with the chief mourner on the right since this is a 'bad time'. It is the victor who should be the chief mourner.

32

Uncommanded

The Tao is eternal and unnameable,
simple, like uncarved wood, a nothing,
yet nothing in the world can command it.
If kings and lords of men could identify with it
everyone would freely submit to them.
Heaven and earth would unite
to drop gentle rain upon them
and everyone would live in harmony,
uncommanded.

But once we carve things out of that simplicity
there is no end to naming the unnameable.
Knowing when to stop is the best we can do.

Look. The Tao is like a great river.
All streams flow into it. It's the ocean.

Notes and commentary
Knowing when to stop. There is a parallel here with the last section of Chapter 28. To preserve order we have to name things, we have to carve out things from their essential unity, but only as far as we need to. To go on cutting is to create too many distinctions and opposites from which we get conflict, contention, argument and disorder, whether we mean by 'cutting' naming and separating things conceptually or, in governing, setting one person or faction above another.

33

Endurance

To understand others is to be wise,
to know oneself is to be enlightened.

Conquering others is a show of force,
conquering oneself is a show of strength.

To be content with what you have is to be rich.

Perhaps you can move mountains,
but only mountains endure.

One who dies but is not lost
is truly immortal.

Notes and commentary
Perhaps you can move mountains. Literally, 'You may be able to get what you want through action, acts of will, but only what is still and non-acting endures.'

One who dies but is not lost. This may, as Waley suggests, refer to the understanding that everything endures in one reincarnated form or other, but I prefer to think it means that one who is in accord with the Tao endures, and understands death as merely phenomenal (see Chapter 16).

34

The Great

The Great Tao is everywhere.
It's here and it's there!
All living things depend on it
and it never deserts them.

It is nothing in particular
but accomplishes everything.

It cares for all and nourishes all
but nothing belongs to it.
It desires nothing.

If you like you can call it
the smallest of the small.
All things return to it
but yet they don't belong to it.
So you could really call it the Great.

In the same way the wise man
who follows the Tao to the end of his days
does not act the part of the great man,
which is how he achieves greatness.

35

Passing By

Whoever holds in his mind
the image of the formless form
will become the one to whom
the world turns
and, turning, will come to no harm.

All is peace and contentment there,
all is at rest.

They who are but passers by
are detained by music
and the taste of things they can't resist.

But the words of the Tao
pass by our lips without taste.

Look at it
and there is nothing to see.
Listen to it
and there is nothing to hear.
And yet, and yet
it never ceases.

36

The Dark Secret

To lessen it
first increase it.
To weaken it
first strengthen it.
To overthrow it
first raise it up.
To take from it
first give to it.

This is the dark secret:
the soft undermines the hard,
the weak overcomes the strong.

Don't disturb the fish
that swim in deep waters.
Don't reveal to the people
the deep workings of the state.

Notes and commentary
There is, in this chapter, both a description of the instruments of the state as they might appear under close analysis, and a parallel with the working principles of the Tao. The state 'undermines' and 'overcomes' challenges to its authority using the same principles. No one needs to know this. Don't disturb it and it will remain harmonious.

37

Nameless Simplicity

The Tao does not act
yet everything is accomplished through it.

If kings and lords of men could identify with it
everyone would freely submit to them.

If the people were then to become restless
I would pacify them
with the uncarved simplicity of the unnameable.

Nameless simplicity breeds no desire
and so all will be at rest
and the world will simply become
enraptured with itself.

Notes and commentary
If kings and lords of men. The wording of this passage is the same as in Chapter 32.

enraptured with itself. I owe this rendering to the translation of Paul Carus.

38

True Virtue

The greatest power
does not possess power
and is therefore most powerful.
Inferior power
holds on to its power
and so is really without power.

The greatest power
does not act
and so its actions are not apparent.
Inferior power is always acting
and so is always on show.

Great benevolence
acts of its own accord
and is never on show.

But 'superior' moral virtue
always needs to be seen as such,
and 'proper' behaviour
always demands recognition.
If you fail to acknowledge it
it will roll up its sleeves
and force itself on you!

When the Tao was lost sight of
its power remained.
When we lost sight of its power
we still had benevolence.
After that, benevolence gave way to moral virtue,
moral virtue to empty forms and proper behaviour.
Nowadays, such grave and decorous behaviour

is merely what is left over of loyalty and good faith
and marks the beginning of disorder to come.

Divining what is to come
is the mere efflorescence of the Tao
and the flowering of ignorance.
And so a great man will concern himself
with the substance of it and not its surface.
He sticks to the plainness of the real
and does not mistake the flower for the fruit.
He chooses the fruit and not the flower.

Notes and commentary
The chapter begins with a discussion of Te, here translated as 'power'. It is not a power that can be possessed or exercised, unlike 'inferior' power which is nothing else. To distinguish the greater from the lesser, we might translate the former as 'virtue' in its older, non-moral meaning, and the latter as power with its current political connotation. It is, says Lao Tzu, the difference between that which acts of its own accord and that which always needs to be noticed and acknowledged. The chapter then goes on once more to castigate superficial social forms of propriety (see Chapters 18, 19, 20) which have come to replace the virtue of Te.

grave and decorous behaviour. I have borrowed these words from Marco Polo, who was describing the aspirations to nobility of the rising middle class of the China of a later age.

Divining what is to come. This last section seems to take its direction from the preceding idea of 'disorder to come'. How do we know what is to come? We know, because we have already been told that what is not in accord with the Tao will naturally come to an end. In other words, losing sight of the harmony of the Tao will lead to disorder. Taoism, as practised, has always contained elements of magic and divination. Here, the fact of prediction seems to be accepted, but at the same time we are told not to mistake these tricks, inherent in the power of the Tao, for its essence.

39

Remaining Whole

These things had unity from the beginning:
Heaven, whole and clear.
Earth, whole and firm.
The spirit of spiritual beings,
the fullness of valleys,
the life in all living things.
Princes and kings had it,
by which all are ruled.
All these arose from an original unity.

Were it not so
the sky might tumble,
the earth crumble,
spirit perish,
the valleys empty,
life burn out.
Princes and kings,
were they not ruled by it
but set themselves on high,
would fall.

Truly is it said
that greatness has humble roots,
the high is founded on the low.
Which is why princes and kings
properly call themselves
orphaned, widowed, worthless.
Isn't this precisely because
greatness is rooted in humility?

Detach a wheel from a chariot
and it's no longer a chariot wheel.

> For those who remain whole
> who you are doesn't matter.
> Jade chimes and stone chimes
> both tinkle.

Notes and commentary
We are here looking back on a supposed golden age when all was still aligned with the wholeness of the Tao. That includes those ideal kings and princes who ruled in accordance with the will of Heaven. The theme of this chapter is lowliness and humility. The argument throughout the Tao Te Ching is that the high is founded on and dependent on the low. A man of worth modestly calls himself unworthy. We must remain whole. A chariot wheel detached from a chariot is nothing at all. When we are whole, when everything remains whole, there is no difference between the integrity of a fine object and an everyday object and the lowly man of Tao does not care either way.

40

Returning

The movement of Tao
is a returning to source.
The Tao works by yielding.

Heaven and earth
and all that is
come into being from being,
but being itself
is born from non-being.

41

The Contrarian Taoist

A perceptive man of learning
when he hears of the Tao
grasps it and puts it into practice.

A middling man
first gets it
and then loses sight of it.

A man of little understanding
laughs out loud at it.
If he didn't laugh at it
it wouldn't be the Tao.

And so we have made these sayings:

Those enlightened by the Tao
appear to be in the dark.
Those most advanced in the Tao
seem to have got it backwards.
Those who have it most straight
seem crooked,
those at the height of their power
lie low, like a valley.
The whiter than white
look shameful.
The most virtuous
seem to lack virtue.
Those most assured of it
are like ones who have lost it.
In them, faithfulness
looks like fickleness.

Greatness in a square
is a square without edges.
Greatness in a pot
is a pot in the making.
Greatness in sound
is the sound of silence.
The greatest form
is formless.

The Tao is hidden
and has no name.
Yet it is just this same Tao
that gives rise to everything
and makes it what it is.

42

The Yin and the Yang

The Tao gives birth to the one.
The one produces two.
Two gives rise to three,
and from three we get the many.
They emerge out of nothing
to become something,
two principles, the yin and the yang,
harmonised in one invisible breath.

No one wishes to be
orphaned, widowed, worthless.
Yet these are what kings and princes
choose to call themselves.
So sometimes to lose is to find
and to find is to lose.

What others have taught I also teach:
'The violent do not die a natural death.'
I shall make this the sound principle of my teaching.

Notes and commentary
The Tao is the unnameable and elusive mother of all things, first giving rise to the 'one' from which the multiplicity of named things arose. They arise from nothing, from the negative principle *yin*, to become something, the *yang*, the negative and the positive, or opposites, harmonised as 'one', as one invisible breath (see the commentary to Chapter 4). The second section reprises passages in Chapter 39. Both the second and third sections appear to have no particular relation to the *yin/yang* passage.

43

Water Wears Out Stone

See how the most immaterial of substances
thunders over the hardest.
The immaterial permeates the impenetrable.

Few there are who understand
the value of a teaching without words,
of acting without acting.

44

To Be Content

Which matters most,
fame
or my own being?
Which is greater,
my own being
or my possessions?
Which hurts most,
to have or have not?

Wanting too much
will cost too much.
The more you have
the more it will hurt
to lose it.

It's not a fault
to be content.
Stop before you begin
and you can go on safely
in this way for ever.

Notes and commentary
Wanting too much will cost too much. There is a price to be paid for greed and lack of generosity, in anxiety, security, the envy of others and the constant threat of loss.

45

The Perfection of the Tao

The most perfect
looks imperfect
but is perfectly useful.
What is full
looks empty
but is never emptied.

The straight
seems crooked,
the skilful
seems clumsy
and its eloquence
stammers.

Movement overcomes cold,
but stillness overcomes heat.
Stillness and perfection –
the rule by which the world is ruled.

Notes and commentary
The thoughts here are similar to those in Chapter 41. The final statement defines the quietist position at the still heart of the Tao.

46

True Contentment

When the world follows the Tao
people give up their carriages
and put their horses out
for carting dung.
When the world is lost to the Tao
the countryside is given up
to breeding war horses.

There is no greater temptation
to crime than desire,
no greater misfortune
than never knowing contentment,
no worse disaster
than wanting more and more.

To be contented,
to know what contentment is,
is to be truly contented.

Notes and commentary
people give up their carriages. They stop dashing about and content themselves with a simple and peaceful life – interpreted metaphorically, they are content to dwell in the stillness of the Tao and not travel far from it. The theme continues in the next chapter.

47

Not Going Anywhere

Without leaving my door
I know what the world is.
Without looking out of the window
I can see what the Tao is.

The farther you go
the less you'll know.

The wise man knows
without going anywhere,
knows what everything is
without looking,
accomplishes everything
without doing anything.

48

Subtracting from the Sum of Knowledge

Whoever studies knowledge every day
learns more and more.
Whoever studies the Tao every day
learns less and less.
He does less and less
until he has learned to do
without doing anything.
This way everything gets done.

A ruler should always rule
by not interfering.
In fact, only by not interfering
is he qualified to rule.

49

One Heart

The wise ruler does not look to his own heart
but finds his heart in the hearts of the people.

'To the good I return goodness,
to those without goodness
I also return goodness
and so they will get to be good.

'To the faithful I return faithfulness,
to those without faith
I also return faithfulness
and so they will get to be faithful.'

He acts in this world disinterestedly,
seemingly indifferent in his actions,
at one with the hearts of the people.
They listen to him and look up to him
and he treats them as his children.

50

At One with Life and Death

Life is a setting out,
death a coming home.

Out of ten men
three are on the outward journey,
three are on their way home,
and three who think
they're on life's journey
are really on their way to death.

Why is this?
Because they are intent on living.

But there is one I hear
who lives his life in such a way
that if along his journey
he should meet a rhinoceros or tiger,
or fall among armed men,
he need not turn away their weapons,
for there is nowhere
that a horn or claw or sword may enter.

Why is this?
Because he is impervious to death.

Notes and commentary
Out of ten men/three. There has been some difference of opinion among translators about the idiom here. Waley reads the text as 'thirteen' – ten plus three – and not, as most other translators do, as 'three in ten', the thirteen being the four limbs and nine orifices of the body. Even when we adhere to a 'three in ten' interpretation, as I have done, a definitive

identification of the three life journeys is difficult. But they have one definite thing in common: they are all intent on life, leading it, preserving it, holding on to it. The implication is that the man of Tao (the tenth man) is at one with life and death (as phenomena) because he is at one with the Tao and its original unity. Again, he does not suffer his mortality (see Chapter 16). He is untouched by the instruments of death because he is impervious to death. By not clinging to life we cannot lose what we don't possess.

51

The Secret of Power

The Tao gives life to the living,
its power nurtures them,
the material world shapes their material forms,
their inborn natures give them their character.

There is not one thing in the world
that does not owe obedience
to the Tao and its power.

But the Tao and its power
do not demand that obedience.
This is just the way things are.

The Tao gives life to them,
its power nourishes them,
brings them up, feeds them,
lets them grow to fulfilment
and looks after them.

To give them their lives
but not own them,
to make them what they are
but lay no claim to them,
to bring them up
without ruling them:
this is the profound secret of power.

52

Living by the Light

The Tao is the mother of all things
from the beginning of the world.
When one knows one's mother
the mother in turn will know her son.
When a mother knows her son
the son in turn will turn to his mother
to keep him safe all his life.

Whoever keeps his mouth shut
and his desires under control
will be free from trouble all his life.
One who has something to say
and interferes with the way things are
will come to a bad end.

To recognise one's insignificance
is to be enlightened,
to be soft is to be strong,
to live by the light
is to find enlightenment
and never be lost,
to be one with what is always so.

Notes and commentary
We have already seen the Tao described as the mother of all things (Chapter 25). Here, the mutual recognition of mother and son is spoken of. It is in fact the fundamental conceit of all religious and spiritual belief that we are not insignificant in the eyes of God, that in recognising God we are in turn recognised, cared for and supported. Similarly, if we know our mother, how could a mother not know her son? We are safe in her (the Tao's) embrace. The Tao is the mother's

breast we have never left (Chapter 20). Yet at the same time, we are 'small', of no significance, just as the Tao is the least of all things and therefore, paradoxically, 'great' (Chapter 34). To know we are nothing, to dwell always in the light of the Tao, is to be enlightened, to be one with the eternal, with the 'always-so' (in Waley's translation).

53

The Way Is Broad and Easy

I don't need to know much
to walk the great way.
I only need to be concerned
about wandering off it.

The great way is broad and easy
but people love to explore the by-ways.

Palaces are full of splendour
but the fields are full of weeds
and the granaries are empty.
They deck themselves out in finery
and carry sharp swords at their sides,
eat and drink to excess
and have no end of wealth.
I call this having the same idea
of one's worth as a robber has.
This isn't the right way.

54

The Measure of the World

What is well planted can't be uprooted,
what is firmly grasped can't be taken from you.

It will not cease,
sustained by ancestral offerings
from generation to generation.

Practise it yourself
and you have the real thing.
Practise it in the family
and its virtue overflows.
Practise it in the village
and its virtue will grow.
Practise it in the state
and its power will flourish.
Practise it in the world
and it will become universal.

By one's own person one measures persons,
by one's family, families,
by one's village, all villages,
by one's state, all states,
by this measure of the world,
the whole world.

How do I know it is so?
By this!

Notes and commentary
Everything must be measured against the Tao. The Tao is firmly planted and everything grows out of it, from the individual through the family, sustained by homage paid to

the ancestors from one generation to the other, adopted by social structures to become the measure of the whole world. I just know this, says Lao Tzu, because I know – this! (the Tao).

55

The Strength of Weakness

One who is grounded in its power
is like an infant.
Poisonous insects do not sting him,
wild beasts do not attack him,
birds of prey do not tear him.
His bones are weak and his muscles soft,
yet his grasp is firm.
He knows nothing of sex
yet he gets an erection.
His spirit is already perfected!
He screams and cries all day
but does not grow hoarse.
His harmony is already perfected!
To know harmony is to know the eternal,
to know the eternal is to be enlightened.
To seek to add to one's life
is to ask for trouble.
Virility is just a show of strength,
and strength eventually wilts.
This is not the way of the Tao
and what does not conform to the Tao
soon comes to an end.

Notes and commentary
The image of the infant is drawn on in several places in the Tao Te Ching (Chapters 10, 20, 28) to illustrate the inherent power of the soft and yielding. One who is grounded in the power of the Tao is like an infant not yet corrupted or tempted by 'knowledge' and yet already 'perfect'. It has to be admitted that the analogy here is taken a step too far. The point of the opening lines would seem to be that the infant does not contend with the world and therefore the world does not

contend with him (see Chapters 22, 66) and he is therefore not in danger from stinging insects, wild beasts and birds of prey. But common experience shows that the innocent are always in danger from the instincts of self-interest in others. The child's screaming and crying is in reality an indefatigable assertion of its own self-interests, and hardly an appropriate illustration of inner harmony.... The last three lines here are the same as those of Chapter 30.

56

One and the Same

Those who know do not speak,
those who speak do not know.

Close your mouth!
Shut the doors!
Take the edge off
your cleverness,
untangle yourself,
dim your light,
be like the dust!

It's all one
and the same
underneath.

To be out of reach,
neither loved nor unloved,
successful nor a failure,
respected nor abused,
is to have the place of honour
in this world.

Notes and commentary
Shut the doors! The gates of the senses.

Cleverness. Literally, sharpness, as of a sword. For a parallel passage, see Chapter 4.

57

Ruling Without Rules

It is said:
The state must rule by the law,
the army act with deception.
I say:
The world is ruled without rules.
How do I know it is so?
By this!

The more rules there are for people to follow
the poorer they become.
The more sharp-witted folk there are among them
the more disordered is the state.
The more inventive people are
the more their strange inventions.
The more laws there are
the more law-breakers.

The wise ruler will say:
I practise the art of doing nothing
and the people of their own accord conform.
By loving quietude
I let the people settle down.
I conduct no business
and the people prosper on their own.
I myself have no desires
and so the people, left alone,
are natural and simple-hearted.

Notes and commentary

By this! By innate knowledge of the Tao. See Chapters 21 and 54.

58

Good and Bad Times

When one governs with restraint
people are content to be contented.
When one is always interfering
the discontented show their discontent.

Unfortunately, unhappiness displaces happiness
as easily as happiness displaces sorrow.
Who knows what the limits are to changeability?
It never ends.
The norms of government are suddenly distorted
and good times turn to bad.
No wonder people are confused – and always have been.

The wise man when he rules
rules squarely
but like a square without corners,
an angle without an edge
that will do no harm,
a straight line not drawn too long,
a light that does not shine!

Notes and commentary
The last section argues for nothing in excess. No sharp edges to his rule, doing nothing to cause harm, not interfering, possessing a hidden inner light (the Tao).

59

The Tao Is the Mother of the State

In governing the people and in serving Heaven
nothing serves better than conserving your resources.
To conserve your resources is to return to the source of power.
Beginning there you can build up your store of power,
and then there is nothing that can't be overcome.
When there is nothing that can't be overcome
then one who has limitless power is fit to possess the state.
In possession of the mother of the state he will endure.
This is to have deep roots and a strong stem,
a long life and a lasting insight into the Tao.

60

Doing No Harm

Govern a great state
the way you cook small-fry.

When the world is governed by the Tao
the spirit of evil no longer haunts the world.
The gods are powerful but do no harm to the people,
and the wise ruler, too, will not harm them.
By doing no harm
the virtue of the Tao is united in them.

Notes and commentary
small-fry. The analogy is with cooking small fishes, such as whitebait, which are lightly dusted and fried with least fuss, meaning: interfere as little as possible and do no harm. The chapter goes on to say that, while the spirit of evil is ever-present, and the gods have power over men, when the world conforms to the Tao and is ruled by it, neither evil spirits nor the gods have any reason to harm the people.

61

Stooping to Conquer

A great state is like a downward flowing river
into which all tributaries run.
It plays the part of the female
whose submissiveness conquers the male
by placing herself under him.
In the same way a great state stoops
to conquer smaller states.
Smaller states submit to a great state
and in their way conquer it.
So, some stoop to conquer,
others stoop and become conquerors.
The only desire of a great state
is to unite the people and provide for them.
The one desire of the smaller state
is to unite with the great state and serve it.
Each in its own way achieves what it desires
but to do this it is essential
that the greater one become the lowlier.

62

The World's Treasure

The Tao is the sacred source of all that is.
It is the treasure of the good man
and the saving grace of the wicked.

There is a market for fine words
and a trade in good deeds
that even the wicked have a share in.

In light of this, when the Son of Heaven
is enthroned as emperor
and the chief ministers invested,
though you send a four-horse chariot
with the gift of a fine jade screen
wouldn't it be as great a gift
to sit still and expound the Tao?

Why did the ancients so value the Tao?
Is it not as the saying is:
'Who shall seek it shall find it
and the wicked shall be saved by it'?
They prized it more than anything in the world.

Notes and commentary
There is a market for fine words. This section and the one that follows it consider the motivations of men. Eloquent speech and doing good deeds can just as easily be a cover for the devious motives of the wicked. In the same way, vying with others to bring the finest gifts at ceremonial occasions is nothing more than buying influence. If you really want to do good, the best gift is to teach the emperor the Tao, which can be taught without fine words and is to be prized above all.

63

Managing Difficulties With Ease

Act without acting,
do without doing,
taste without tasting.
Treat the great as small
and the many as few.
Return hatred with virtue.

Take on the difficult
while it is easy,
venture great things
while they are small.

The world's difficulties
were surely easy at the beginning,
the world's great affairs
began small.

The wise man
never plays the role
of a great man
but just the same
achieves great things.

As promises made lightly
are not to be trusted
what is taken to be easy
will turn out to be difficult.
By considering the easy
as the beginning of difficulty
nothing ever becomes difficult.

64

Ends and Beginnings

What is already at peace
is most easily kept at peace.
What has not yet happened
is most easily prevented.
What is weakest
is most easily broken.
What is few in number
is most easily dispersed.

Deal with things before they happen,
sort things out before they turn into a mess.

A tree too big to get your arms around
grew from a little root.
A nine-storey tower arose brick by brick.
A journey of ten thousand miles
began with the first step.

When you act upon something
you spoil it.
When you grasp at something
you lose it.
The wise man does not act
so spoils nothing,
grasps at nothing
so loses nothing.

People often fail in their business
just as they are about to bring it to conclusion.
To succeed you need to be as careful of the end
as you are of the beginning.

The wise man desires
what others neglect.
He places no value on rare things
and as for learning
he prefers un-learning.
He returns to what others have neglected
and lets everything develop of its own accord.
But he must never dare to act!

Notes and commentary
This chapter continues the theme of managing affairs while they are still manageable so that they do not grow into difficulties and complexity. Here, the principle is applied to statecraft and to worldly affairs. That principle is *wu-wei*, non-action. By not interfering, by preferring simple ways to cleverness, the wise man or wise ruler returns (and returns the people) to what has been neglected, the Tao, from which all things develop of their own accord if left alone.

65

Profound Simplicity

In ancient times
those who practised the Tao
did not use it to make the people wise
but to keep them simple-hearted.

Clever people are always difficult to govern.
Clever people in government are an affliction
and a country is better off without them.
He who understands these two facts
sets a standard and a model to follow.
To always have them in mind
is to understand how deep runs
the mysterious power of the Tao.
Its depth is truly profound and far-reaching,
underlying the commonality of things
and restoring their original harmony.

Notes and commentary
The argument, here and throughout the Tao Te Ching, is that world is essentially simple – simple at the beginning, and simple to the end, if we can avoid imposing our own ideas upon it. From our modern scientific perspective, the emergence of complexity in matter and in evolution is entirely explainable from simple beginnings. As the world has become more complex, we have lost sight of its profound simplicity. Governing is no longer about meeting people's essential needs, but fulfilling all their wants. Those in power are greedy, those without power greedily demand it. Eric Hoffer, the American longshoreman philosopher, was sceptical of the value of the intellectual in society. One of the chief problems, he said, 'is how to provide an outlet for the intellectual's restless energies yet deny him power.' (1967

CBS interview with Eric Sevareid.) In Hoffer's book, *The True Believer* (1951) he says: 'A man is likely to mind his own business when it is worth minding. When it is not, he takes his mind off his own meaningless affairs by minding other people's business.'

66

High and Low

The reason rivers and seas
are greater than the tributaries that flow into them
is that they are good enough to lower themselves,
and it is this that makes them lords of their tributaries.
In the same way a wise man
who would make himself a great lord over the people
will speak humbly to them and lead from behind them.
Yes, he is above them but he does not burden them,
and by leading from behind he does not get in their way.
And so the people are happy to raise him over them
without fearing the burden of oppression.
And because he has no argument to make with anyone,
no one in the world comes into conflict with him.

67

I Have Three Jewels

This Tao of mine everyone calls great
resembles nothing in particular.
It is great precisely for that reason.
If it had to be something in particular
what a nothing it would be!

I have three jewels.
I treasure them and keep them safe.
The first is compassion,
the second is living modestly,
the third not putting myself forward.

If you have compassion you can be fearless.
If you are sparing you can be generous.
If you do not put yourself first
you can be the means by which others prosper.

But when people are fearless but merciless,
when they squander their resources,
abandon restraint and put themselves to the front,
surely they are bound to die.
In battle they should fight with mercy
and defend themselves with compassion.
It is, after all, only the compassion of Heaven that
saves them.

Notes and commentary
the compassion of Heaven. Everything is fated, all eventualities are ruled by Heaven (see Introduction). It can therefore only be the compassion of Heaven that allows one to be saved (in battle). We should act as Heaven acts.

68

The Will of Heaven

A great warrior is not warlike.
He fights without anger
and conquers without seeking vengeance.

To lead the people
you must submit to them.

This is the art of avoiding conflict,
of making the most of people's abilities
and conforming to the will of Heaven.

From the beginning of time
this has always been
the perfect way to be.

69

No Enemy

One who understands the art of war says:
I did not invite it,
I am simply a guest.
I would not advance an inch,
but rather retreat a foot.

This is called:
going off to war without marching,
threatening without raising a hand,
opposing without enmity,
arming without arms.

In war there is nothing more fatal
than despising the enemy.
If we despise the enemy
we throw away our three jewels.

When two equal armies clash
the one with no enemy will win.

Notes and commentary
This chapter continues the critique of war. It is not a plea for pacifism but shows how the principles of Taoism should shape the minds and attitudes of those who have no choice but to face the realities of enmity and aggression. There is an art to war. Passion, hatred, despising the enemy, dismissing and underestimating the enemy are not part of it. We are detached participants who do what must be done. We should not sacrifice the 'three jewels' identified in Chapter 67 by abandoning compassion, squandering resources, seeking glory for oneself. Hence, given two equal but opposed forces the army that holds on to its integrity and does not give way to vengeful anger will come out on top.

70

The Hidden

My words are very easy to understand
and put into practice
yet no one in the world understands them
or puts them into practice.

My words have an ancestor
and my deeds have a lord.
If no one understands this
no one will understand my teaching.

What I teach is understood by only a few
which only makes it more valuable.

I am like one who goes around
in home-spun garments
hiding a jewel under his coat.

Notes and commentary

My words have an ancestor. His words and actions come directly from the Tao. Without first having that understanding neither these words nor my actions will be understood. The Tao, we have learned, is wordless and actionless, so what use are words and deeds without that primal understanding? This is the deep paradox of Lao Tzu's teaching of the Tao: it can't be spoken of so speaking of it has no value except as the acknowledgement of what we already know. I think this explains the concision and the allusive nature of the text of the Tao Te Ching: it is understood by those who already understand it, but decoding it alone will not provide an understanding. It is the same paradox we come across frequently in the literature of Zen Buddhism and the Zen *koan*, and it is what Lao Tzu points to by his oft-used self-explanatory exclamation, By this! The Chinese poet Han Shan also found the right phrasing for this same paradox:

> *No use looking for it –*
> *turn around and it's there!*

Knowledge of the Tao is rare and therefore more valuable, like a jewel hidden under the commonest of appearances, unlike the ostentatious display of those attached to worldly treasures. It's this, not that.

71

Enigmatic Lucidity

To know the unknowable
is a high achievement.
Not to know
what can be known
is a kind of sickness.
Only when we become sick of sickness
do we stop being sick.
The one who knows
is not sick
because he's sick of sickness.

Notes and commentary
This is a syntactically difficult chapter, playing on the word for 'sickness'. Fortunately, in English we use the word in the two senses we need at this point: to be sick, as an affliction, and to be sick *of*, in the sense of fed up with. The meaning is that to know the Tao is indeed a high achievement. It can be known by following the teaching. Since it can be known, not to know it is a kind of sickness. We are, as it were, shut off from it, quarantined. Not until we find the will to know the Tao, not until we are sick of our sickness of not knowing, can we escape our sickness.

Enigmatic lucidity. I have taken this happy phrase from Waley's commentary on this chapter.

72

The Burden of Life

It is when people least expect
what they fear
that what they feared
descends on them.

Don't fence them in.
Don't make their lives a burden.
They will not weary of life
if you do not burden them.

The wise ruler prefers
self-knowledge to self-regard,
self-contentment to self-love,
rejecting one for the other.

Notes and commentary
Paul said: *For when they shall say Peace and safety; then sudden destruction cometh upon them.* [1 Thes.5:3] Chapter 72 begins a sequence of statements advising the ruler not to impose his power on the people, not to oppress them and make their lives more burdensome than the mortal burden they already bear. What they most fear (death) will overtake them in its own course, without cause.

rejecting one for the other. See Chapter 12.

73

The Net of Heaven

The courage to act
can lead to death.
The courage not to act
can preserve life.
Acting and not acting
are sometimes right,
sometimes wrong.

Who knows what the will of Heaven is
in what it chooses?
Even the wise man
finds it hard
to fathom a reason.

The Tao of Heaven
never argues
yet always wins the argument,
never asks
but has a way of answering,
can't be summoned at will
and yet it comes.
It is slow
but sure.

The net of Heaven is vast
and its mesh is wide
yet nothing is ever lost.

Notes and commentary
There is no formula for escaping bloodshed. In times of impending conflict, to act, to take up arms, can lead to death. Resist the temptation to act, and disaster will overtake you

because you did not act. This is an interesting slant on *wu-wei*, non-action. By non-action we do not mean refusing to act when you need to act. It is not an absolute position. It is a puzzle. Sometimes we are right, sometimes wrong, and for all the right reasons. Who knows what is fated by Heaven? Here, the Tao and Heaven are given an equivalence. It does what it does the way it does. Everything is held in its power, and our own attempts to sort things out happen within, and not outside, its net.

74

The Executioner

The people are not actually afraid of death,
so what use is it to threaten them with execution?
If we could make them afraid of death
I could seize and kill anyone who stepped out of line
and then no one would dare.

There has always been an executioner,
the bringer of death.
To take his place yourself
is, as it were, to usurp the role
of the master carpenter who does the cutting.
Whoever takes the master's place
is in danger of cutting his own hand.

Notes and commentary
In Chapter 72 we are led to believe people are afraid of death, which can take them by surprise, and in Chapter 73 we are told that both action and non-action can lead to death, a danger we try to avoid yet whatever we do it sooner or later catches up with us. In contrast, Chapter 74 appears to begin with a statement that people are not afraid of death. I think what is meant here is that capital punishment is not the deterrent it is purported to be. It punishes people for their offences, but it has never permanently succeeded in discouraging people from committing those offences. If it worked, then the fact that anyone at any time could be seized and put to death would prevent every sort of dissent. Clearly this has never been so. Fear of death does not keep everyone in order, the light hand of the enlightened ruler does that, as we have learned throughout the teaching of the Tao Te Ching. We already have an executioner: death is willed by Heaven. It is not your role to act as though you acted

with the hand of Heaven, and if you do then you, a clumsy interfering amateur and not the master of fate, are likely to cut your own hand.

75

Too Much

The people starve
when their rulers
overburden them with taxes.

The people become difficult to govern
when the government
interferes too much.

They hardly give death a thought
for life itself consumes their lives.

Better to care less for life
than care too much.

Notes and commentary
Life is a burden to the people when those above them overtax them for their own benefit, fence them in with laws and punishments to keep them under control. They are so consumed by the effort of simply staying alive that there is no time to reflect on death. If life is a burden, what is there to regret about losing it? The self-indulgent rulers are the ones who actually cling to life for their own pleasures, so in a way the enslaved people, who make light of death, are morally superior to their rulers.

76

The Strongest Tree Is Marked for Felling

Living, a man is soft and pliant.
Dead, he is hard and rigid.
The grass, the trees,
while they live, bend with the breeze.
Dead, they are dry and hard.

The hard and rigid
belong to death,
the soft and pliant
belong to life.

It follows that those
whose strength lies in arms
cannot conquer,
that the strongest tree
is marked for felling.

The great and strong fall,
the soft and pliant rise.

77

Evening Things Out

The Tao of Heaven
is like the stretching of a bow:
its high point is brought down,
its low point raised up.
It evens things out
by taking from those who have much
and giving to those who have little.

That is the way of Heaven:
to reduce those with much
and increase those with little.

But the way of men is not like this.
It takes from those who have little
for the benefit of those who have much.
How can creating wealth for yourself
be the best way to serve the world?

The wise ruler creates wealth
but desires nothing for himself.
He deserves merit but asks for none.
What need has he
to draw attention to himself?

Notes and commentary
Left alone, the world finds its equilibrium. This is the way of Heaven. When you stretch a bow, the high point is brought down to meet the low point which is brought up by this stretching. But men try to pile up wealth and power for themselves with no sense of equity. This is the corruption and self-interest we see in rulers everywhere, yet the whole purpose of government is to create wealth for the people,

quite selflessly. Merit will naturally accrue to one who does not seek it.

78

The Paradox of Weakness

In this world
there is nothing softer or gentler
than water
yet no one
pitting himself against the hard
and the strong can do better.
Nothing better exemplifies
how weakness defeats strength
and the gentle overcomes hardness.
Everyone knows this
yet no one acts in this way.

A wise man has said:
'Whoever takes upon himself the sins of this world
is its master.
Whoever lays claim to the world's wickedness
is its ruler.'
Such is the paradox of words truly said.

Notes and commentary
The ideal ruler is submissive, and accepting of the great responsibility he has inherited – to the extent that he accepts the evils, failures and the 'dirt' of the world as his own. We have a habit of blaming others, blaming a past administration, and walking away. But the first step in sorting out the world's evils is to acknowledge them as yours.

79

The Impartiality of Tao

Even when you've reconciled
disputing parties
some resentment will remain.
How to deal with this?
The wise man will know
what his debtor owes him
but will not pursue the debt.
The man of Tao respects his obligations,
when others press their claim.

The Tao of Heaven is never partisan
and so always aids the impartial man.

Notes and commentary
The analogy is with the method of reconciling disputes over contracts, where each party holds his half of the agreement as either creditor or debtor. The man of Tao is like the creditor, who knows what is owed to him but does not pursue his claim and will leave it in abeyance and not become the source of renewed contention. He has the power and the right to intervene and make his claim, but he chooses not to. This is Heaven's way. As we have learned above (Chapter 77) Heaven evens things out and does not lend its power to one above another.

80

Let Us Go Back

Let us go back
to small states with few people
where, if you offered them
a hundred new inventions,
they would have no use for them.

They would be content to live and die there
and not move from place to place.

Even if there were boats and carriages
they would have no reason to go anywhere.

If they had weapons and armour
they would have no reason to take them up.

They would go back
to using knotted cords for writing.
They would enjoy simple food and clothing,
content with their huts
and happy in their country ways.

If there were neighbouring countries
in sight of each other,
so close you could hear cocks crowing
and dogs barking, even so
people would grow old and die where they live,
and no one would come
and no one would go.

81

There Is No Argument

True words are not sweet,
sweet words are not true.

The good and true man
does not argue with words.
Those who dispute with words
do not know the good and true.

There is wisdom without learning
and learning without wisdom.

The wise man keeps nothing for himself.
He gains more for himself
by working for others.
The wise ruler gains most
when he gives everything to the people.

The Tao of Heaven is benevolent
and does no harm.
The Tao of wisdom is to act
and not to argue.

Notes and commentary
The Tao Te Ching ends as it began: the true way is not a matter of words whose truth we can argue about. Knowledge is not the same as wisdom. The Tao of wisdom is to act – but of course to act in accord with the Tao, which acts without acting, and in this way, as with the way of Heaven, we can do no harm and come to no harm.

www.ingramcontent.com/pod-product-compliance
Lightning Source LLC
Chambersburg PA
CBHW051807040426
42446CB00007B/562